Theodore Roosevelt

Progressive President

Tamara Orr Staats

Boston, Massachusetts
Chandler, Arizona
Glenview, Illinois
Upper Saddle River, New Jersey

Illustrations
Opener, 1, 2, 3, 4, 8, 10, 11, 15 Dan Bridy; 13 Joe LeMonnier.

Photographs
Every effort has been made to secure permission and provide appropriate credit for photographic material.
The publisher deeply regrets any omission and pledges to correct errors called to its attention in subsequent editions.

Unless otherwise acknowledged, all photographs are the property of Pearson Education, Inc.

Photo locators denoted as follows: Top (T), Center (C), Bottom (B), Left (L), Right (R), Background (Bkgd)

Opener: Prints & Photographs Division, LC-USZC4-11867/Library of Congress; 1 Prints & Photographs Division, LC-USZC4-11867/Library of Congress; 5 Prints & Photographs Division, LC-USZ62-113665/Library of Congress; 6 Prints & Photographs Division, LC-USZ62-11990/Library of Congress; 7 Prints & Photographs Division, LC-DIG-pga-01946/Library of Congress; 9 Stereograph Cards Collection, Prints & Photographs Division, LC-DIG-stereo-1s02050/Library of Congress; 12 Prints & Photographs Division, LC-USZC4-11867/Library of Congress; 14 Medioimages/Photodisc/Thinkstock.

ISBN-13: 978-0-328-67627-9
ISBN-10:   0-328-67627-6

3 4 5 6 7 8 9 10 V0FL 15 14 13 12

A President Who Loved Nature

Have you ever visited one of our country's beautiful national parks, such as the Grand Canyon? If so, you owe Theodore "Teddy" Roosevelt some thanks. It is partly because of him that we have national parks and national forests.

This is the story of Teddy Roosevelt. He was the popular twenty-sixth president of the United States. Roosevelt worked to make life better for American citizens. He helped make the United States a world power. And he also worked to protect millions of acres of American **wilderness** for all to enjoy.

Early Years

Theodore Roosevelt was born to a wealthy New York City family on October 27, 1858. He was a frail and sickly child. He suffered from an illness called asthma.

Today, there are many ways to help people with asthma. But when Roosevelt was young, not much could be done. His father told Roosevelt that if he worked hard, he could "make his body." When his father built him a gym in their home, Roosevelt exercised and exercised. It worked! He grew so strong he became a wrestler in college.

As a sickly child, Roosevelt spent a great deal of time indoors. He loved collecting and studying objects from nature. His collection included snake skins, stuffed animals, and even the skull of a seal.

As an adult, Roosevelt became a hunter and added to his collection. The story of an unsuccessful hunting trip became famous. Its organizers tied an old bear to a tree to give Roosevelt something to shoot. But Roosevelt refused. It was cruel, he said. Then a cartoon about the trip ran in newspapers. Soon after, stores began to sell stuffed bears called "teddy bears."

College and Marriage

Roosevelt studied at Harvard University. There he became interested in **politics**. Roosevelt was only 23 when he won his first public office.

A friend from Harvard had introduced Roosevelt to his future wife, Alice Lee. They were married in 1880. But four years later, she died after giving birth to their daughter. Sadly, Roosevelt's mother also died on the same day.

Later, Roosevelt married his childhood sweetheart, Edith Carow. Together, they raised six children.

Roosevelt out West

Roosevelt was extremely sad after losing his wife and mother. In order to get away from everything, Roosevelt decided to move west.

For two years, he lived the life of a cowboy and a rancher in North Dakota. Roosevelt discovered the beauty of that part of the country. His love of nature and wildlife grew even stronger.

Rough Riders

When Roosevelt returned home, he also returned to politics. First, he became head of New York City's police department. Then, he was named the assistant secretary of the U.S. Navy.

In 1898, the United States declared war on Spain. One battleground was Cuba, an island country south of Florida. Roosevelt wanted to fight. He organized a group of cowboys and ranchers from his days in the west. They were called the Rough Riders.

On July 1, 1898, Roosevelt led the Rough Riders into victory in one of the war's most important battles. It was also one of Roosevelt's proudest moments. The United States won the war.

Roosevelt and the
Rough Riders in Cuba

Political Life

Roosevelt was a hero when he came home from the war. He ran for governor of New York and won. However, many politicians didn't like him. That's because instead of going along with their ideas, Roosevelt had his own. Before he took office, big businesses often made unfair demands on their workers. Roosevelt wanted to change that. He helped limit the number of hours government workers could be asked to work. He also made sure teachers in New York were paid fairly.

Leaders began to notice Roosevelt. In 1900, President William McKinley asked Roosevelt to run as his vice president. Roosevelt's energy and pounding fist drew huge crowds wherever he spoke. People loved listening to him. McKinley and Roosevelt won the election.

During his time as vice president, Roosevelt became more and more interested in world events. Increasingly, Roosevelt began to believe that the United States needed a stronger army and navy.

A McKinley-Roosevelt campaign poster

President

On September 6, 1901, a terrible event occurred. After giving a speech, President McKinley was shot. He died a week later. Vice President Roosevelt became president. At age 42, he was the youngest person to hold the office.

As president, Roosevelt began to push his **progressive** ideas. He called for **regulation** of businesses. While he believed that the government could help businesses, he also believed that government should make laws to protect workers as well.

A Square Deal

President Roosevelt spoke out for a "square deal." He wanted government to be fair to everybody. He used this approach during a **strike** by coal miners in 1902. The strike threatened to cause a coal shortage. The president stepped in to help end it. He got the two sides to sit down and talk. With his help, they were able to come to an agreement.

Speak Softly

Roosevelt believed that the United States should be a world power, a leader in the world. He was famous for saying that a president must "speak softly and carry a big stick." He meant that a powerful country, such as the United States, should be willing to use force if necessary. However, it should always try to talk through differences first. Roosevelt worked hard to keep the country's army and navy strong.

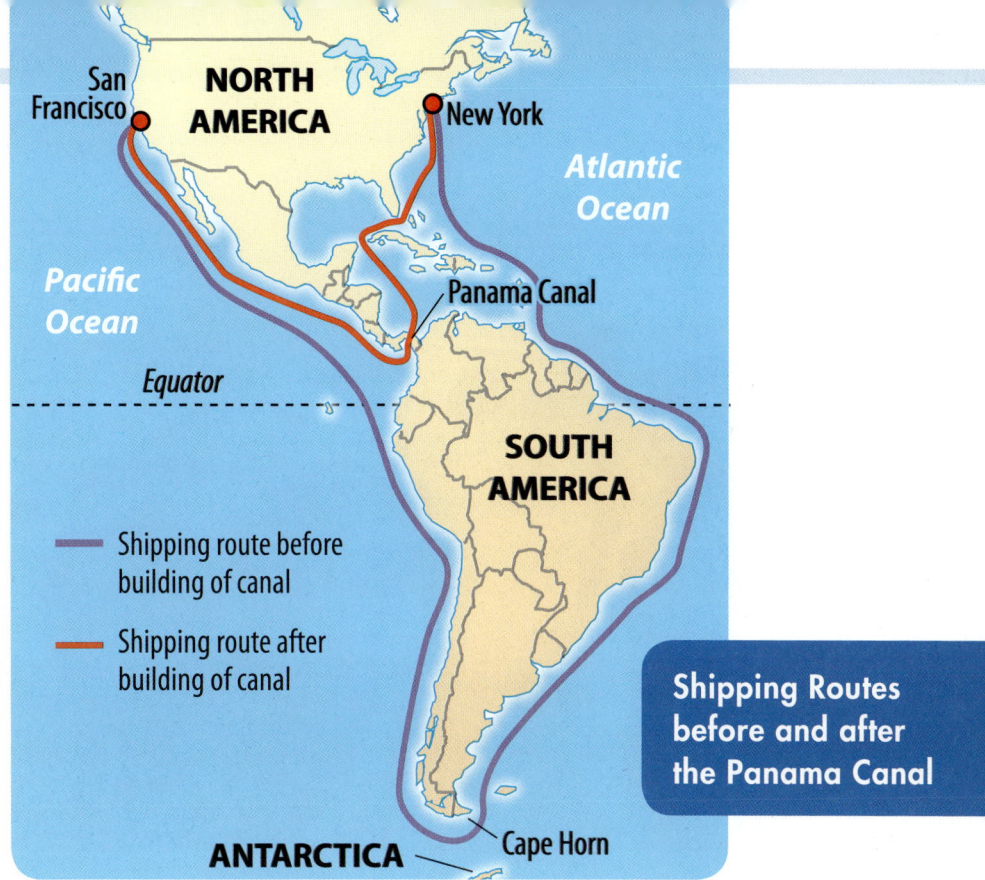

San Francisco

NORTH AMERICA

New York

Atlantic Ocean

Pacific Ocean

Panama Canal

Equator

SOUTH AMERICA

— Shipping route before building of canal

— Shipping route after building of canal

Shipping Routes before and after the Panama Canal

ANTARCTICA — Cape Horn

Panama Canal

For years, people had dreamed of creating a shortcut that ships could use to travel between the Atlantic and Pacific oceans. At the time, if a ship sailed from New York to California, it had to sail around the tip of South America. If a **canal** were dug through Central America, it would allow ships to have a much shorter trip.

President Roosevelt wanted this canal to be built, and he helped make it happen. The Panama Canal took nearly 10 years and 30,000 workers to build. It was finally finished in 1914.

Conservationist

When Roosevelt was president, people were becoming more aware of dangers to the country's **environment** and to the animals that lived there. One example was the bison, an animal that had once roamed the West in huge numbers. Now it was nearly gone. Hunters had killed nearly all of them.

Roosevelt knew the West and loved the bison. He wanted to save them and preserve the nation's environment. As president, Roosevelt set aside 5 national parks and more than 100 national forests. He became known as the first **conservationist** president.

Remembering Roosevelt

Roosevelt left office in 1909. He died in 1919, at the age of 60. Today, many people consider Teddy Roosevelt to be one of our country's greatest presidents. He certainly had a big personality, and it was matched by big accomplishments. He helped make the country stronger and fairer. He also worked to make sure that the wilderness would be protected for all Americans.

Glossary

canal a waterway that people dig across land to connect bodies of water

conservationist a person who works to manage or protect nature

environment the surroundings people live in, including all living and nonliving things

politics activities connected to government

progressive wanting to improve or reform government and business

strike an action by workers in which they stop working as a way to get better pay or working conditions

regulation the act of controlling something

wilderness wild land where people do not live